Jane Austen

WRITERS IN BRITAIN

Nicola Barber

Published by Evans Brothers Limited
2A Portman Mansions
Chiltern Street
London W1M 1LE

© Evans Brothers Limited 1999

First published 1999

Printed at Oriental Press, Dubai, U.A.E.

ISBN 0 237 51743 4

British Cataloguing in Publication Data

Barber, Nicola
    Jane Austen. - (Writers in Britain)
    1. Austen, Jane, 1775-1817 - Biography - Juvenile literature
    2. Women novelists, English - 19th century - Biography -
    Juvenile literature 3. Novelists, English - 19th century -
    Biography - Juvenile literature
    1. Title
    823.7

This book is dedicated to my parents. N.B.

Acknowledgements

Consultant – Jean Bowden, Jane Austen Memorial Trust

Editor – Su Swallow
Designer – Ann Samuel
Production – Jenny Mulvanny
Picture Research – Victoria Brooker

For permission to reproduce copyright material, the author and publishers gratefully acknowledge the following:

Cover (Main image) Robert Harding Picture Library (inset) Corbet/Everett **page 5** Robert Harding Picture Library **page 6** Musee Carnavalet, Paris/Bridgeman Art Library, London **page 7** (top) Mary Evans Picture Library (bottom) Mary Evans Picture Library **page 8** e.t. archive **page 9** (top) Mrs E Fowle/Jane Austen Memorial Trust (JAMT) (bottom) Mary Evans Picture Library **page 10** (top) JAMT(bottom) Private Collection/Bridgeman Art Library **page 11** (top from left) JAMT, Mrs E Fowle/JAMT, JAMT, Mrs E Fowle/JAMT, Dr B Willan/JAMT (bottom) Corbis/Everett **page 12** (top) Hampshire Record Office (bottom) City of Bristol Museum and Art Gallery/Bridgeman Art Library **page 13** (top) Chawton House, Hampshire/Bridgeman Art Library (bottom) Collections/Brian Shuel **page 14** JAMT **page 15** (top) Mary Evans Picture Library (bottom) Mallett & Son Antiques Ltd., London/Bridgeman Art Library **page 16** (top) Corbis/Everett (bottom) Corbis/Everett **page 17** (top) Mary Evans Picture Library (bottom) Corbis/Everett **page 18** (top) National Gallery of Scotland, Edinburgh/Bridgeman Art Library (bottom) Corbis/Everett **page 19** Corbis/Everett **page 20** Victoria and Albert Museum, London/Bridgeman Art Library **page 21** (top) Private Collection/The Stapleton Collection/Bridgeman Art Library (bottom) Mary Evans Picture Library **page 22** (top) e.t. archive(bottom) Collections/George Wright **page 23** (top) Private Collection/Bridgeman Art Library (bottom) Collections/Alain le Garsmeur **page 24** Collections/Robin Weaver **page 25** (top) Private Collection/The Stapleton Collection/Bridgeman Art Library (bottom) Collections/Michael Allen **page 26** (top) Robert Harding Picture Library (bottom) Jane Austen Society/JAMT **page 27** (top) JAMT (bottom) Corbis/Everett

Contents

Events at home and abroad

*J*ane Austen was born in 1775 and died at the age of 41 in 1817. According to her nephew, James Edward Austen-Leigh, her life was 'uneventful'. Whether, in fact, Jane Austen's personal life was quite as crisis-free as her nephew portrayed it, is open to question (see page 12). What is certain is that these were times of revolution and change. The French Revolution in 1789 led to a series of wars between France, Britain and other European powers. In Britain, there was a different and more gradual kind of change taking place which we now call the Industrial Revolution. It is often noted that Jane Austen ignores such world issues in her novels, but revolution and change did have an impact upon the society that she knew so well and wrote about so accurately.

> **"** *Of events her life was singularly barren; few changes and no great crisis ever broke the smooth current of its course.* **"**
> *Memoir of Jane Austen* by her nephew James Edward Austen-Leigh (1870)

This painting depicts the event that started the French Revolution: the storming of the royal fortress called the Bastille, in Paris, 14 July 1789.

Revolution in France

In July 1789, the French people rose up against their king, Louis XVI, and the nobility, in protest at the monarchy's extravagance and the burden of crippling taxes. The king and queen were executed in 1793.

In the years that followed, different groups struggled for power in the new French Republic. In 1799 an officer in the French army, Napoleon Bonaparte, took control of the government. Napoleon was a brilliant administrator and military commander. He wanted to expand his empire and set about conquering neighbouring countries. This led to a series of wars, known as the Napoleonic Wars. For Britain, the two most notable dates were 1805 and 1815. In 1805, the combined French and Spanish fleets were destroyed by the British fleet under the leadership of Lord Nelson at the Battle of Trafalgar. This victory gave control of the seas to Britain for the rest of the Napoleonic era. In

1815, Napoleon was finally conquered by forces from many European countries under the leadership of the Duke of Wellington, at the Battle of Waterloo in Belgium.

The mad king

For most of the people of Britain, revolution and wars were a distant, if ever-present, concern. Two of Jane Austen's brothers were at sea in the navy during the Napoleonic Wars, so she was well aware of battles and victories. She was also interested in events closer to home. King George III was well-loved by his subjects, but suffered from bouts of illness and madness that started in 1788. His eldest son and heir, the Prince of Wales, was less well liked. He was extravagant, always in debt, and often drunk. In 1795 he married Princess Caroline of Brunswick despite the fact that he had secretly married his mistress, Maria Fitzherbert, ten years earlier.

In this 18th-century cartoon, the Prince of Wales gazes at portraits of pretty women while a German messenger tries to interest him in Princess Caroline of Brunswick.

In 1811 the old king's fits of madness became so bad that the Prince of Wales was appointed as Prince Regent. He celebrated with a lavish party to which he did not invite his wife, the unfortunate Caroline. Jane Austen was not impressed with the Prince's behaviour and wrote about Princess Caroline in a letter of 1813: 'Poor Woman, I shall support her as long as I can, because she is a Woman, & because I hate her Husband...'

Industrial beginnings

The Industrial Revolution began in Britain during the 18th century. Britain was rich in natural resources such as coal and iron. Other raw materials were imported from Britain's overseas colonies. There were advances in technology, with machines such as the spinning jenny leading to the mechanisation of weaving and cloth-making. Another major development, the steam engine, provided the power necessary to drive these new machines.

In 1767, James Hargreaves invented the spinning jenny.

Royal dedication

Jane Austen may have disapproved of the behaviour of the Prince Regent, but when it was made known to her that he admired her novels and that she was 'at liberty' to dedicate the next one to him, she had little choice but to comply. She suggested the straightforward wording 'Emma, Dedicated by Permission to HRH The Prince Regent' to her publisher, but he had other ideas and a much longer dedication finally appeared in the front of *Emma*:

❝*To His Royal Highness the Prince Regent, this work is by his Royal Highness's Permission, most respectfully dedicated, by his Royal Highness's dutiful and obedient humble servant, the author*❞

Britain in the 18th century

An 18th-century painting of the country estate of the Earl of Coventry. The grounds were landscaped by Capability Brown (see page 24). The ownership of land was very important in Britain at this time.

These words of the famous writer, Dr Johnson (1709-84), illustrate the importance of class in 18th-century Britain. His phrase describes a structure in which everyone was considered to have a place, from the land-owning aristocrat to the poorest vagabond. This generally accepted ideal was thought to be vital for the continuation of peace and prosperity, but was being challenged by thinkers from the Americas and Europe. It provided the framework for Jane Austen's novels, in which she portrays the subtle distinctions between the different ranks and stations of society (see page 20).

Landowners

The ownership of land was very important in 18th-century Britain. At the top of the social scale were aristocrats and nobility who were born into positions of wealth and power. They usually owned large estates in the country, as well as a house in London. Below them came the gentry who were also landowners. Their social position varied according to the size of their estates and their houses. Although their land was usually farmed by tenants, many landowners took a keen interest in the running and improvement of their estates (see page 24). Thomas Coke of Norfolk improved sheep, pig and cattle breeds and introduced new methods of farming. He also held huge sheepshearing meetings at his estate in Holkham which attracted people from all over Europe. Even King George III set up model farms on his land, and was knowledgeable about stock breeding and crop growing.

Jane Austen herself could claim aristocratic connections through her mother, but her family was by no means wealthy. Her father was a country clergyman, with a parish in Steventon in Hampshire. Her family belonged to the professional class which included clergymen, lawyers, and officers in the army and navy. However, one of her brothers, Edward, was adopted by rich relatives and eventually inherited large estates in Kent and Hampshire (see page 11).

A miniature of Jane's father, George Austen.

The 'middling sort'

The 18th-century phrase, the 'middling sort' is often used to describe the people who were neither gentry, nor of the professional class, but who were not dependent on manual labour for their income. These were people who ran local businesses, such as the miller, or the innkeeper. Below them were skilled craftspeople such as blacksmiths or clockmakers. Then came labourers, and the mass of people who lived in real poverty, reliant on charity or the workhouse for their living. Jane Austen knew her duty to the poor families living in her father's parish at Steventon. In a letter of 1798 she wrote: 'Of my charities to the poor since I came home, you shall have a faithful account. – I have given a pair of Worsted Stockings to Mary Hutchins, Dame Kew, Mary Steeven & Dame Staples; a shift to Hannah Staples, & a shawl to Betty Dawkins...' This may not sound very generous, but until Jane Austen earned money from writing, she was given only £50 a year for clothes and other personal expenses.

Social mobility

Although the social order provided a framework for 18th-century life in Britain, people were not necessarily trapped in the class to which they were born. There was a great deal of social mobility, and the key to mobility was money. As the Industrial Revolution progressed, a new group of people became established who had made their fortunes not from inherited wealth or from land, but from trade and manufacturing. Jane Austen was well aware of the arrival of this new class of gentry, and depicted the snobberies attached to 'old' and 'new' money in several of her novels.

Riot and rebellion

Although there was no revolution in Britain like the one in France, there was unrest in many towns in the late 18th and early 19th centuries. Bad harvests and the Napoleonic Wars were the cause of several riots about food shortages. There was also resistance to the changes of the Industrial Revolution. In 1811 and 1812, the Luddites (named after their leader Ned Ludd) broke factory machinery and caused disturbances all over the north of England. Troops were sent to put down the rebellions, and 17 Luddites were eventually executed for their part in the unrest.

Luddites attack factory machinery.

The Austen family

Jane's father, the Reverend George Austen

*J*ane Austen was the seventh child in a family of eight children. Her father, George Austen, was a clever and well-educated man who had been a Fellow at St John's College, Oxford, before marrying and becoming a country parson. Her mother, Cassandra Leigh, was a practical, down-to-earth woman, with a sparkling wit. Jane had five elder brothers and one younger. She also had one sister, her beloved Cassandra. The two were inseparable throughout their lives. As their mother remarked: 'if Cassandra's head had been going to be cut off, Jane would have hers cut off too...'

The parsonage in Steventon was a lively place. Jane's parents ran a boys' school for the sons of squires and other local gentry, so Jane grew up surrounded by boys and boys' pursuits. Although George Austen educated his sons at home, Cassandra and Jane were sent away to two boarding schools. At the first school, both girls nearly died of an infectious fever. They were rescued by Mrs Austen and an aunt, who then herself caught the fever and did die. Luckily, the second school was a healthier place, although Jane and Cassandra seemed to be taught very little. They had dancing lessons, learned basic spelling and French, practised their needlework and possibly took part in plays.

Life was more fun at home where her brothers organised theatrical events. One Christmas they fitted up a barn as a theatre, with painted scenery. Their cousin, Eliza de Feuillide (see box) was staying with the Austens, and took leading roles in their plays. Jane Austen was too young to take an active part, but must have watched, fascinated, by all the theatrical business around her.

Jane's mother, Cassandra Austen

A silhouette of Jane's beloved sister, Cassandra, made in about 1809

Eliza de Feuillide

Eliza de Feuillide was an exotic creature in the Austens' world. As a young woman, Eliza's mother (Jane's father's sister) had been shipped off to India to look for a wealthy husband. Eliza was born in India, and herself married a French count. She was pretty and glamorous and loved to flirt with Jane's grown-up brothers, James and Henry. In 1794, her husband was executed in Paris by the revolutionaries. Eliza eventually married Henry, and she remained a close friend of Jane Austen until her death in 1813.

Jane's brothers:

James

Henry

There is no existing picture of George, the Austen's second son.

Edward

Francis

Charles

Jane's brothers

The Austen brothers were a successful bunch. The exception was the second son, George, who was born with a disability and lived apart from the family. The eldest, James, went to Oxford and became a parson like his father. Henry, Jane's favourite brother, was a lively and charming character. He also went to Oxford University, then became a banker. Henry used his influence to get Jane's novels published, and often dealt with publishers on her behalf (see page 14). When his business went bankrupt he, too, became a parson.

Edward, although lacking James's intellect and Henry's wit, was in some ways the luckiest of all the Austens. He was adopted by some distant cousins, Mr and Mrs Thomas Knight of Godmersham, Kent. The Knights were childless, and when Thomas Knight eventually died, Edward took his name and inherited his wealth. Both Jane and Cassandra were frequent visitors at their brother's large country house in Godmersham.

Francis and Charles were in the navy, and both were involved in the Napoleonic Wars. They were eventually both to become admirals, but this was long after Jane Austen's death. From them, Jane knew much about the details of navy life, and naval characters appear frequently in her novels, particularly in *Persuasion*.

The navy

Jane Austen's approval of the navy and its ways is obvious in her novels. Her naval characters, such as Captain Wentworth and the Crofts in *Persuasion*, are usually fine, upright, no-nonsense people. This admiration is voiced in *Persuasion* by Louisa who: '... burst forth into raptures of admiration and delight on the character of the navy – their friendliness, their brotherliness, their openness, their uprightness...'

The 'uneventful' life of Jane Austen

Marriage is central to Jane Austen's novels, but neither she nor Cassandra ever married. Cassandra fell in love with a penniless parson called Tom Fowle. They became engaged, but did not marry as neither had enough income to set up home together. In 1795, Tom Fowle was appointed chaplain to an army regiment and sailed for the West Indies. He died there of yellow fever, the news reaching the distraught Cassandra in 1798.

Jane Austen's love life has excited much interest. She delighted in going to balls and in dancing, and she herself recounts in a letter the fun of flirting with a visitor to Hampshire, 'her Irish friend' Tom Lefroy. The day before Tom Lefroy was due to leave for Ireland she wrote to Cassandra:

> **66** *At length the Day is come on which I am to flirt my last with Tom Lefroy, & when you receive this it will be over – My tears flow as I write, at the melancholy idea.* **99**

It is known that Jane accepted one proposal of marriage, from a family friend called Harris Bigg-Wither. But, after a tormented night considering her decision, she took back her acceptance. The advantages that marriage to Harris Bigg-Wither would have brought were considerable: an estate in Hampshire, wealth and comfort for herself and her family. But, as she was later to write in advice to a niece: 'Anything is to be preferred or endured rather than marrying without Affection.'

Tom Lefroy was a law student in Ireland. In 1795-6 he visited his uncle in Hampshire and met Jane Austen at a ball.

A gathering at the Clifton Assembly Rooms in Bristol. This picture shows the dress and behaviour of the gentry in the late 18th and early 19th centuries.

On the move

In 1801, Mr and Mrs Austen decided to move from the country parsonage in Steventon which had been Jane Austen's home for over 25 years. It was at Steventon that Jane had written the first drafts of her three earliest novels, *Sense and Sensibility*, *Pride and Prejudice* and *Northanger Abbey*, although none had yet appeared in print. The family took lodgings in Bath, and went on extended tours to visit relations, and to various resorts in the West Country. During this time, Jane Austen almost stopped writing. No one knows why, but it was undoubtedly difficult to find the peace and solitude necessary to sit and write, and there was also possibly a sense of insecurity and depression. She only resumed her work when Edward offered his mother and sisters (her father died in 1805) a permanent home at Chawton, on his Hampshire estate.

It was at Chawton that she wrote her three later novels, *Mansfield Park*, *Emma* and *Persuasion*. But in the spring of 1816, she started to feel unwell. She battled against her illness to finish off *Persuasion*, and even started a new novel, *Sanditon* in January 1817. In May 1817, Jane and Cassandra took lodgings in Winchester in order to be nearer the doctors who were treating her. She died in July and was buried in Winchester Cathedral.

Chawton House and Park in Hampshire. Jane's brother, Edward, inherited this estate after the death of Thomas Knight, his adopted father.

Scandal

In 1799, a very peculiar event occurred in the Austen family. Mrs Leigh-Perrot, Mrs Austen's wealthy sister who lived in Bath, was charged with shoplifting. A shop assistant found a piece of lace caught up in the string of her brown paper parcel after she had left the shop, and a few days later she was confined to the jailor's house in Ilchester awaiting trial. This was the cause of much scandal and gossip in Bath and beyond. It was also a very serious situation as, if found guilty, Mrs Leigh-Perrot could face the death penalty. Mrs Austen wrote to her sister offering to send Jane and Cassandra to keep her company in prison! Luckily for them, Mrs Leigh-Perrot refused. And thankfully for Mrs Leigh-Perrot she was found not guilty at her trial.

8 College Street, Winchester, the house where Jane Austen died on 18 July 1817

Writing novels

Chawton Cottage, Jane Austen's home from 1809 until just before her death in 1817

*I*n his *Memoir of Jane Austen*, her nephew James Edward Austen-Leigh described how his aunt worked on her novels at Chawton Cottage. '... she had no separate study to retire to, and most of the work must have been done in the general sitting-room, subject to all kinds of casual interruptions... She wrote upon small sheets of paper which could be easily put away, or covered with a piece of blotting paper...'. Her family, Cassandra and Henry in particular, were supportive. Cassandra undertook many of the daily chores around the house, leaving Jane relatively free to write. And it was Henry who encouraged her, and arranged and paid for the publication of her first novel *Sense and Sensibility* in 1811. This novel was published anonymously, as were *Pride and Prejudice* in 1813, *Mansfield Park* in 1814 and *Emma* in 1815. After his sister's death, Henry arranged publication of *Northanger Abbey* and *Persuasion*, which appeared in 1818 with a biographical note written by Henry revealing the author's name and history.

> 66 *I think I may boast myself to be, with all possible vanity, the most unlearned, & uninformed female who ever dared to be an authoress.* 99
>
> Letter to James Stanier Clarke, 1815

Success and excess

The novels were a great success. From the publication of *Sense and Sensibility* Jane Austen received £140, the first money she had earned. She received favourable reviews, and came to the notice of the Prince Regent (see page 7). But her success changed her daily life very little.

Anonymous authors

The number of women authors increased dramatically towards the end of the 18th century. Writing was the only profession open to women; the Church, the law, medicine, the army and the navy were still entirely male worlds. However, even being published could be a risky business for a woman. Women were supposed to be retiring and modest, but getting published demanded a certain amount of self-publicity. This is why many women authors published their first novels anonymously, or under a male pen-name. It is also why Henry Austen emphasised his sister's 'sweet' and 'religious' nature in his biographical note (see page 26) about her.

She chose not to meet other literary figures of the day, although we know that she read and admired the writings of Dr Johnson (1709-84) and the poet William Cowper (1731-1800). She also knew the works of other women authors such as Ann Radcliffe (1764-1823), Frances Burney (1752-1840) and Maria Edgeworth (1767-1849). In *Northanger Abbey*, she famously defends the novel at the same time as making fun of the excesses of one particular type of writing – the Gothic novel.

Terror in the Abbey

The Gothic novel revelled in everything that was sentimental and sensational. Its heroines swoon and weep; its settings are craggy castles with secret hiding places; there are suspicious deaths and mysterious messages. During Jane Austen's lifetime, the best-known novel in this style was the *Mysteries of Udolpho* by Ann Radcliffe. It is this very book that Catherine Morland and Isabella Thorpe are reading with such relish in *Northanger Abbey*:

> ❝ *...But my dearest Catherine, what have you been doing with yourself this morning? – Have you gone on with Udolpho?"*
> *"Yes, I have been reading it ever since I woke; and I am got to the black veil."*
> *"Are you indeed? How delightful! Oh! I would not tell you what is behind the black veil for the world! Are not you wild to know?"*
> *"Oh! Yes, quite; what can it be? – But do not tell me – I would not be told upon any account. I know it must be a skeleton...* ❞

The novelist Maria Edgeworth. She published many successful novels including *Castle Rackrent* and *Belinda*.

Strawberry Hill in Twickenham was one of the earliest examples of the Gothic in architecture. The house was owned by the writer Horace Walpole. He transformed it from a small coachman's cottage into a Gothic castle complete with battlements and turrets.

When Catherine goes to stay at Northanger Abbey itself, she is disappointed that the building is not more dark and forbidding. But her fertile imagination, fired by her lurid reading, soon leads her to the suspicion that General Tilney must have murdered his wife. It takes Henry Tilney's gentle rebuke to remind her that real life is not the same as fiction: 'Dear Miss Morland, consider the dreadful nature of the suspicions you have entertained. What have you been judging from?'

Jane Austen's heroines

In all of Jane Austen's novels, the plot centres around one or two main female characters. Elizabeth Bennet in *Pride and Prejudice* is one of five sisters, but she possesses the liveliest wit and the acutest mind of all of them. Catherine Morland in *Northanger Abbey* is young and impressionable. Elinor and Marianne Dashwood in *Sense and Sensibility* are opposites; Elinor reasonable and responsible, Marianne ruled only by her heart and senses. Fanny Price in *Mansfield Park* is an unlikely heroine – poor and put-upon by her grand relations, she nevertheless shows herself to have the finest judgement of all around her. Emma Woodhouse is the only one of Jane Austen's heroines to have the book named after her, and she is a larger-than-life character: intelligent, witty – and a snob. In *Persuasion* the last of Jane Austen's heroines, Anne Elliot, has thrown away her own happiness with a mistaken decision before the action of the novel even starts.

Jane and Elizabeth Bennet, the eldest of the five Bennet daughters in the BBC TV adaptation of *Pride and Prejudice*

Jane Austen's books are sometimes thought of as cosy stories about privileged characters who spend their lives going to balls and visiting each other's country homes. But a closer look at Austen's heroines soon reveals that they all have to struggle with problems and difficult issues before the inevitable happy ending. In fact, the characters in the novels who are portrayed as easy-living are usually shown to be selfish and indolent. In *Mansfield Park*, Lady Bertram spends most of her time either asleep on the sofa or doting on her little pug dog: 'Lady Bertram, sunk back in one corner of the sofa, the picture of health, wealth, ease and tranquillity, was just falling into a gentle doze...'. But she fails to exercise proper control over her wayward children, and when disaster strikes she is unable to cope without Fanny's support.

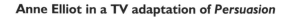

Anne Elliot in a TV adaptation of *Persuasion*

An illustration from an early 20th-century edition of *Sense and Sensibility*. Marianne blushes as she is teased by the indiscreet Mrs Jennings.

Raising the blushes

Observing

Jane Austen grew up in a large and loving family, but her position in life allowed her to observe those around her with some detachment. She did not marry and therefore lacked the status that a husband brought. She was not rich, and spent most of her time at home with her sister and mother. Yet she often visited her rich brother in Kent, and knew the ways of a wealthy country house. She also went to stay with Henry and Eliza in London, mixing with a cosmopolitan crowd at their parties. All this provided experience for her novels, although she did not base her characters directly on individual people.

Emma Woodhouse

At first sight, it may not seem that Jane Austen's most famous heroine, Emma, has to struggle with many difficulties. In the very first sentence of the novel we are told that she is 'handsome, clever, and rich, with a comfortable home and a happy disposition'. But her self-confidence leads her to interfere with other people's lives, and to make some serious errors of judgement. In one episode, she makes fun of a silly but blameless character, Miss Bates. Mr Knightley, who has heard Emma's rudeness with amazement, takes her to task for her improper behaviour and Emma realises the full impact of her words: 'Never had she felt so agitated, mortified, grieved, at any circumstance in her life. She was most forcibly struck. The truth of his representation there was no denying. She felt it at her heart. How could she have been so brutal, so cruel to Miss Bates!' Emma is forced to examine her own faults and shortcomings, and only then can the novel draw to its happy conclusion.

> " *To strive with difficulties and to conquer them is the highest human felicity; the next is to strive and deserve to conquer them.* "
>
> Dr Johnson, from *The Adventurer III*

Emma, in a film version of the book

Marriageableness

All Jane Austen's heroines end up married, and we are left in no doubt that these are good marriages. We know that Jane Austen accepted and then turned down an offer of marriage because she did not love the man concerned (see page 12).

Similar questions of judgement crop up throughout her novels. Her heroines must struggle for the right kind of marriage, even if this means disappointing others. Meanwhile, there are plenty of examples of bad marriages all around them.

'The Bride at her Toilet', painted in 1838. Marriage is a central theme in all of Jane Austen's novels.

Charlotte Lucas and the disagreeable Mr Collins in the BBC TV adaptation of *Pride and Prejudice*

Marrying for connections and situation

Pride and Prejudice announces its main theme in the very first sentence of the book: 'It is a truth universally acknowledged, that a single man in possession of a good fortune, must be in want of a wife.' Mrs Bennet's only concern throughout the novel is to see her daughters married well (to ensure that they will have a roof over their heads as the family home will go to Mr Collins on Mr Bennet's death). Both Elizabeth and Jane do, eventually, marry the right men. But the most shocking marriage in the book is that of Elizabeth's friend, Charlotte Lucas. She accepts a proposal from the snobbish and foolish Mr Collins only three days after that gentleman had proposed to Elizabeth herself! Elizabeth finds it difficult to come to terms with this news, even after Charlotte's explanation: ' "I am not romantic you know. I never was. I ask only a comfortable home; and considering Mr Collins's character, connections, and situation in life, I am convinced that my chance of happiness with him is as fair, as most people can boast on entering the marriage state." '

Charlotte Lucas accepts Mr Collins's proposal because she knows that in her limited circle she is unlikely to receive a better one in material terms. She is prepared to forgo any expectation of real happiness for 'connections and situation in life'. Although Jane Austen portrays Charlotte Lucas as a sympathetic character who knows the implications of what she is doing when she makes her decision, this is exactly what her real heroines cannot bring themselves to do, and why they must struggle with the consequences.

Making the right marriage

The consequences for Fanny Price are painful. Her position as a poor relation living on the charity of her aunt and uncle at Mansfield Park is a difficult one. When she receives a proposal of marriage from the dashing and well-connected Henry Crawford, it is assumed by her uncle, Sir Thomas Bertram, that she will accept. But Fanny has seen enough of Henry to doubt his moral worth and, secretly, she is in love with Edmund, Sir Thomas's second son. This leads to the following exchange:

> "Am I to understand," said Sir Thomas, after a few moments silence, "that you mean to refuse Mr Crawford?"
> "Yes, Sir."
> "Refuse him?"
> "Yes, Sir."
> "Refuse Mr Crawford! Upon what plea? For what reason?"
> "I – I cannot like him, Sir, well enough to marry him."
> "This is very strange!" said Sir Thomas, in a voice of calm displeasure.

Of course, Fanny is proved right. Henry runs off with Sir Thomas's married daughter, and in the end Fanny marries Edmund. But Fanny's fairytale ending is a result of her holding on to what she knew to be right, even at times of greatest pressure.

A happy conclusion: Elinor Dashwood marries Edward Ferrars at the end of a film version of *Sense and Sensibility*.

The importance of money

Two fashionable ladies take the air in a phaeton. In *Northanger Abbey*, Catherine Morland is taken reluctantly for a drive in a similar type of carriage by John Thorpe.

> 66 *... two thousand a-year is a very moderate income... A family cannot well be maintained on a smaller. I am sure I am not extravagant in my demands. A proper establishment of servants, a carriage, perhaps two, and hunters, cannot be supported on less.* 99
>
> Marianne in *Sense and Sensibility*

Jane Austen is very particular to give the incomes of her characters although in this example she is making fun of Marianne, as a clergyman and his family, for example, could live comfortably, with two servants, on just £400. Money is an important indicator of status, but equally as important is the way in which money is used. The responsibilities that go with being a landowner are underlined in all the novels. Sir Walter Elliot of Kellynch Hall is excessively proud of being a baronet, and acutely aware of the dignity of his position as a landowner, but with little sense of his moral duties. He is forced to vacate his grand estate because of debt, and the description of his leaving Kellynch Hall makes it clear that he has not been a good landlord: 'The party drove off in very good spirits; Sir Walter prepared with condescending bows for all the afflicted tenantry and cottagers who might have had a hint to shew themselves.'

In contrast, Jane Austen's two most famous heroes, Mr Knightley in *Emma*, and Mr Darcy in *Pride and Prejudice*, are shown to be good landlords. They both have money, but they use it well. Mr Knightley takes an active interest in the running of his estate. He is also concerned with the well-being of his tenants.

Elizabeth Bennet's first impression of Mr Darcy is of his excessive pride, and this is proved by his behaviour to her when he proposes marriage for the first time. But a visit to his estates in Derbyshire shows her another side of his character. Her astonishment increases as the housekeeper of Pemberley sings her master's praises: ' "He is the best landlord, and the best master... There is not one of his tenants or servants but will give him a good name. Some people call him proud; but I am sure I never saw anything of it..." '

A design for a 'modern living room' by Humphry Repton (see page 25). People with money commissioned interior and garden designs to show off their wealth.

New money

The responsibilities that came with wealth were important for maintaining the social order. However, Jane Austen was also well aware of the existence of a new class of wealthy people, those who had made their fortunes through trade (see page 9). The subtle distinctions between wealth derived from long associations with land, and wealth from trade is illustrated by Emma's confusion about how she should treat some new arrivals to the Highbury circle, the Coles: 'The Coles had been settled some years in Highbury, and were very good sort of people – friendly, liberal, and unpretending; but, on the other hand, they were of low origin, in trade, and only moderately genteel.' When the Coles announce their intention to hold a party, Emma is determined that she will refuse. But she swallows her pride when she discovers that all her friends are less inclined to such snobbery, and that she alone will be left at home in 'solitary grandeur'. She finally admits that 'considering everything, she was not without inclination for the party'.

In *Pride and Prejudice*, the difference between Mr Darcy and Mr Bingley is also carefully noted. Mr Darcy's £10,000 a year comes from his Derbyshire estate which has been in his family for many generations. Mr Bingley's family, however, have made their money more recently from trade, and he is now looking for a country house to buy so that he, too, may live the life of a landed country gentleman.

Poverty

As the wealthiest inhabitant of Highbury, Emma is well aware of her duties to the less well-off. Emma may have her faults, but Jane Austen is careful to show her compassion when dealing with the poor: 'They were now approaching the cottage, and all the idle topics were superseded. Emma was very compassionate; and the distresses of the poor were as sure of relief from her personal attention and kindness, her counsel and her patience, as from her purse.' In contrast, Sir Walter Elliot in *Persuasion* cannot see beyond his own vanity. When Anne Elliot announces her intention of visiting an old school friend, Mrs Smith, who has fallen on hard times, he disapproves entirely. His disapproval is based on the fact that Mrs Smith lives in an unfashionable part of town, and that she is untitled, poor and an invalid: ' "...who is Miss Anne Elliot to be visiting in Westgate-buildings? – A Mrs Smith. A widow Mrs Smith, – and who was her husband? One of the five thousand Mr Smiths whose names are to be met with everywhere. And what is her attraction? That she is old and sickly...'

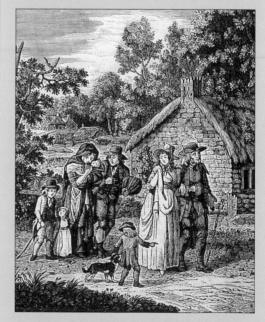

Country people are evicted from their village in this 18th-century illustration

Taking the waters

The Pump Room, Bath. It is in this room that Catherine Morland first meets Isabella Thorpe in *Northanger Abbey*.

*J*ane Austen's dislike of Bath is well known. She may have enjoyed visiting this fashionable town to take the waters with her parents, but when she was forced to move there permanently in 1801 (see page 13) her surviving letters leave little doubt that she found it an unpleasant place to have as her home. She wrote to Cassandra: 'The first view of Bath in fine weather does not answer my expectations; I think I see more distinctly thro' Rain, – The Sun was got behind everything, and the appearance of the place from the top of Kingsdown, was all vapour, shadow, smoke and confusion.' A later comment underlines her boredom with the endless social round: 'Another stupid party last night...'

> 66 *She disliked Bath and did not think it agreed with her – and Bath was to be her home.* 99
>
> Anne Elliot's view of Bath in *Persuasion*

The Royal Crescent in Bath was designed by John Wood the Younger (son of John Wood the Elder – see box on page 23) and built in 1767-74.

Spas and watering places had become increasingly popular throughout the 18th century. Bathing in or drinking natural spa water that contained particular minerals was thought to be effective for a wide range of ills. Spa towns such as Buxton, Harrogate, Scarborough and Tunbridge Wells, and later Cheltenham, became popular centres, but the most fashionable of them all was Bath. It became an essential part of a gentleman's year to be seen there during the season. A whole new town was designed and built during the 18th century, including the crescents and terraces that still stand today.

Jane Austen set two of her novels partly in Bath: much of *Northanger Abbey* takes place in the town, and part of *Persuasion*. In *Northanger Abbey*, the heroine, Catherine Morland, first meets Mr Tilney in the Lower Assembly Rooms, and makes friends with Isabella Thorpe in the Pump Room. There is no doubt that Catherine Morland finds Bath an exciting place to be, but she is merely a visitor. The daily round of visits, parties and theatre trips is in such contrast to her quiet life at home that she is delighted by all she sees. In *Persuasion*, however, Sir Walter Elliot is persuaded to rent out his country house and move to Bath in order to save money. Jane Austen's most mature heroine, Anne Elliot, dreads Bath as a home.

Bath

The Georgian city of Bath was designed by the architect John Wood the Elder, backed by his patron Ralph Allen. The main building was carried out in the 1730s, '40s and '50s. Wood wished to revive the splendours of an ancient Roman city, with large assembly places, wide streets, and a 'Grand Circus'. However, the story goes that the city council got so fed up with John Wood and his plans that they named four streets after him: Be Street, Quiet Street, John Street, Wood Street.

At the seaside

Another way of taking the waters that became fashionable towards the end of the 18th century was sea bathing. In fact, many doctors of the time not only recommended bathing in sea water but also drinking it. The craze for seaside cures was given the royal seal of approval by the Prince of Wales. When he visited Brighton he liked the town so much that he had his own Pavilion built there.

Jane Austen tried out the delights of sea bathing at Lyme Regis. In fact, as she herself remarked, she rather overdid it on one occasion: 'The Bathing was so delightful this morning... that I believe I staid in rather too long, as since the middle of the day I have felt unreasonably tired.' She used her explorations of Lyme Regis to provide the setting for a dramatic incident in *Persuasion*, when Louisa Musgrove injures herself on the long sea wall, called the Cobb. Her appreciation of this seaside town is obvious from the detailed description of Lyme in the novel: 'the Cobb itself, its old wonders and new improvements, with the very beautiful line of cliffs stretching out to the east of the town, are what the stranger's eye will seek; and a very strange stranger it must be, who does not see charms in the immediate environs of Lyme to make him wish to know it better...'

Sea bathing became very popular at the end of the 18th century.

The sea wall, called the Cobb, in Lyme Regis

Improving the view

Tours of the Peak District (above), Lake District, Scottish Highlands and other wild places became very popular in the late 18th and early 19th centuries.

Picturesque principles

On his travels through Britain, the Reverend Gilpin went in search of 'the grand natural scene' which to his eyes was 'superior to the embellished artificial one'. Although impressed by the magnificence of raw nature, for a landscape to be 'correctly picturesque' Gilpin considered that practised viewers should apply the principles of painting to it: 'In such immense bodies of rough-hewn matter, many irregularities, and even many deformities, must exist, which a practised eye would wish to correct.' By reshaping a mountain or adding a forest, either in the mind's eye or on canvas, it was possible for human taste and judgement to improve on nature.

For those of an adventurous nature, an alternative to visits to spa towns or the seaside was a trip to the wild and rugged landscapes of the Lakes or the Peak District. Such landscapes had become increasingly popular in the 18th century, largely due to the influence of the Reverend William Gilpin who published a series of books describing his travels in such picturesque parts of Britain. In fact, this movement became known as the Picturesque, and it affected both literature and art.

Jane Austen probably visited the Peak District in the summer of 1806 while staying with some cousins in Staffordshire. In *Pride and Prejudice*, she sends her heroine, Elizabeth Bennet, on a sightseeing tour of Derbyshire. Her interest in the Picturesque, and her knowledge of Gilpin's books is also clearly shown in *Northanger Abbey*. Gilpin suggested that the viewer should borrow terms from the world of painting, and apply them to the natural landscape. On a walk in the countryside around Bath, Henry Tilney and his sister busy themselves 'viewing the country with the eyes of persons accustomed to drawing, and decided on its capability of being formed into pictures.' Later, Henry gives the enthusiastic Catherine Morland a lesson on how a landscape should be viewed in the Picturesque manner: 'He talked of fore-grounds, distances, and second distances – side-screens and perspectives – lights and shades...'

Improving the estate

There were many who loved rugged landscapes, but did not want the discomfort of travel to appreciate them. Many wealthy landowners in the 18th century introduced some of 'wild nature' into their own estates. Many employed the garden designer, Lancelot Brown, who was nicknamed Capability Brown because of his habit of saying, "There are great capabilities here." Out went formal gardens, and in came natural curves, clumps of trees, waterfalls, lakes and half-hidden ruins. All was designed to look as natural, yet as tasteful, as possible.

A view of Longleat House from Prospect Hill by Humphry Repton. This illustration is taken from Repton's *Observation on the Theory and Practise of Landscape Gardening* (published in 1803) in which he set down his ideas about improving the landscape.

> " *It wants improvement, ma'am, beyond any thing. I never saw a place that wanted so much improvement in my life...* "
>
> Mr Rushworth in *Mansfield Park*

The subject of improving the estate is debated at length in *Mansfield Park*. Jane Austen had seen at first hand the work of Capability Brown's successor, Humphry Repton. Like many other writers in the 18th century she questions the craze for 'improvement'. These changes were purely ornamental and used up vast amounts of money and labour. Through the characters in *Mansfield Park*, Austen implies that this is not consistent with the responsibilities of estate ownership (see page 8). Mr Rushworth is a keen improver and plans to employ Repton to work on his estate at Sotherton. He will cut down an avenue of old trees to open up the view from his house. Fanny bemoans such an idea: ' "Cut down an avenue! What a pity!" ' Later in the book, Henry Crawford tries to persuade Edmund to improve the parsonage that will soon be his home. ' "The farm-yard must be cleared away entirely, and planted up to shut out the blacksmith's shop. The house must be turned to front the east instead of the north... You must make a new garden at what is now the back of the house...". But Edmund's reply, and the response that we assume Jane Austen approves of, is: ' "I have two or three ideas also... and one of them is that very little of your plan... will ever be put in practice." '

Out of sight

The ambitions of a landowner to improve his estate sometimes had far-reaching effects for his long-suffering tenants. In Dorset, the entire town of Milton Abbas was removed between 1771 and 1790 to make way for the Earl of Dorchester's new house and park. The Earl did not wish to see his tenants, and had new cottages built well out of sight of his grand mansion.

The village of Milton Abbas, built by the Earl of Dorchester for his evicted tenants.

Changing views

This picture of Jane Austen is taken from the engraving made by her nephew, James, for *A Memoir of Jane Austen*, published in 1870.

Much has been written about Jane Austen's life and her character. Only two years after her death, *Persuasion* and *Northanger Abbey* were published with a biographical note by her brother, Henry. In this note he stresses his sister's good character, her sweetness of temper and her unshakeable Christian faith. For a woman to publish under her own name was still considered a risky business (see page 14), so it is not surprising that Henry wished to emphasise his sister's good character.

Throughout her life, Jane Austen was an avid letter writer. Many of these letters were to her sister, Cassandra, with whom she corresponded frequently when they were apart. The letters tell us much about the Austens' daily lives, about concerns with health, about journeys, about new dresses and trimmings for bonnets. They also allow us to see Jane Austen's active and witty mind busily observing those around her. However, there are gaps in the letters. After her sister's death, Cassandra destroyed some of Jane's letters to her. The missing letters seem to coincide with times of difficulty and stress in Jane's life: the Bigg-Wither proposal (see page 12), or the move from Steventon (see page 13). Possibly they contained personal criticisms or references which Cassandra did not want a wider public to read.

In 1870, Jane Austen's nephew (son of James Austen) wrote a *Memoir* of his famous aunt. Like Henry, he was keen to emphasise her uneventful life and her good, Christian character. He quoted from her letters, but left out parts that he felt might cause offence, or spoil the favourable portrayal of his aunt. For example, he quotes much of a letter that Jane wrote to Cassandra in 1814, but omits the amusing line: 'Give my Love to little Cassandra, I hope she found my Bed comfortable last night & has not filled it with fleas.' ('Little' Cassandra was Charles Austen's daughter.)

Restoring Jane Austen

The popularity of Jane Austen's novels grew during the 19th century, particularly after the publication of the *Memoir*, and has continued throughout the 20th century. There have been some dissenting voices, however. Charlotte Brontë wrote

Charles Austen gave these topaz crosses to his sisters. Jane's cross is on the left, Cassandra's on the right

'The Passions are perfectly unknown to her; even to the Feelings she vouchsafes no more than an occasional graceful but distant recognition;'.

A similar criticism was made by D. H. Lawrence, who called Jane Austen 'thoroughly unpleasant'. More recent writers have seen Jane Austen as a link between the ordered values of the earlier part of the 18th century and the beginnings of a new emphasis on the individual reflected in the Romantic movement at the beginning of the 19th century. Publication of the complete (uncut) letters, and several new biographies have also renewed interest in Jane Austen's life, and shown that she was not quite the saintly, sweet spinster aunt that James Edward Austen-Leigh portrayed, but a real-life person with a devastatingly accurate eye and cutting wit.

> 66 *That young lady had a talent for describing the involvement and feelings and character of ordinary life which is to me the most wonderful I ever met with.* 99
>
> Walter Scott, *Journal*

A letter from Jane Austen to her lifelong friend and companion, her sister Cassandra. In it she discusses the weather, and a book she is reading.

Darcymania

Jane Austen's novels continue to be as popular as ever in the late 20th century. In particular, they translate well on to the screen – both television and film. Recent adaptations of *Pride and Prejudice*, *Sense and Sensibility*, and *Emma* have been huge box office successes. The television adaptation of *Pride and Prejudice* provoked a huge interest because of the prominence given to the character Mr Darcy, played by Colin Firth. For a time, Darcymania seemed to grip the nation. However, no screen version can ever do justice to Jane Austen's text, and so it is to the books that Jane Austen fans return, reading and re-reading her six novels many times over.

Mr Darcy (Colin Firth) and the new Mrs Darcy (Jennifer Ehle) leave the church after their wedding at the end of the BBC TV adaptation of *Pride and Prejudice*.

	1764	Marriage of George Austen and Cassandra Leigh 26 April
	1765	James Austen born 13 February
	1766	George Austen born 26 August
	1767	Edward Austen born 7 October
	1768	Austen family move to Steventon
	1171	Henry Austen born June 8
	1773	Cassandra Austen born 9 January
	1774	Francis Austen born 23 April
	1775	Jane Austen born 16 December
Adam Smith *The Wealth of Nations*	**1776**	
	1779	Charles Austen born 23 June
	1783	Edward Austen adopted by Mr and Mrs Knight Jane and Cassandra sent away to school in Oxford and Southampton
	1784	Jane and Cassandra sent to school in Reading
Prince of Wales marries his mistress, Maria Fitzherbert, secretly and illegally	**1785**	
King George III's first serious illness	**1788**	
Start of French Revolution, Paris, 14 July	**1789**	
Thomas Paine *The Rights of Man*	**1790-1**	
Mary Wollstonecraft *A Vindication of the Rights of Woman*	**1792**	
King Louis XIV of France executed by guillotine 21 January Queen Marie-Antoinette of France executed by guillotine 16 October War with France	**1793**	
Ann Radcliffe *The Mysteries of Udolpho*	**1794**	Eliza de Feuillide's husband executed by guillotine in Paris
Prince of Wales marries Caroline of Brunswick	**1795**	Tom Fowle goes to West Indies Jane Austen starts work on *Elinor and Marianne* (*Sense and Sensibility*)

	1776	Jane Austen starts *First Impressions* (*Pride and Prejudice*)
	1797	Tom Fowle dies in West Indies Eliza de Feuillide marries Henry Austen
	1798	Jane Austen starts *Susan* (*Northanger Abbey*)
Beginning of Napoleonic Wars	**1799**	Mrs Leigh-Perrot is arrested for shoplifting in Bath
	1801	The Austen family move to Bath
	1802	Harris Bigg-Wither proposes to Jane Austen, is accepted and then rejected next morning
Peace of Amiens – brief respite in wars	**1802-3**	
	1803	Austens visit Lyme Regis
Napoleon declares himself Emperor of France	**1804**	
Battle of Trafalgar 21 October	**1805**	George Austen (father) dies
	1806	Austens visit Stoneleigh Abbey in Warwickshire
	1809	Austens move into Chawton Cottage
Prince of Wales appointed Prince Regent	**1811**	Publication of *Sense and Sensibility* Jane Austen starts *Mansfield Park*
Luddite Rebellions	**1811-12**	
	1813	Eliza Austen (de Feuillide) dies Publication of *Pride and Prejudice*
	1814	Jane Austen starts *Emma* Publication of *Mansfield Park*
Battle of Waterloo 18 June	**1815**	Jane Austen starts *Persuasion* Publication of *Emma*
	1816	First signs of illness. Cassandra and Jane move to Winchester in May
	1817	Jane Austen dies 18 July Jane Austen is buried in Winchester Cathedral 24 July
Mary Shelley *Frankenstein*	**1818**	Publication of *Northanger Abbey* and *Persuasion*

Index

Further reading

There are hundreds of books about Jane Austen. Some of the most useful for more detailed study of her novels and her life are:

Penguin editions of the novels all have an extensive introduction. In addition the Penguin *Persuasion* and *Northanger Abbey* include Henry Austen's biographical note. Penguin also publish Critical Studies on all the Austen novels.

Preface Books: A Preface to Jane Austen by Christopher Gillie provides a very useful first look at the background to Jane Austen's novels.

The Cambridge Companion to Jane Austen edited by Edward Copeland and Juliet McMaster has a useful collection of essays for the more advanced student.

Jane Austen A Life by Claire Tomalin is an excellent and readable biography.

Jane Austen by David Noke

Jane Austen's Letters Collected and edited by Deirdre Le Faye. Complete collection of the letters with extensive notes.

Jane Austen and the English Landscape by Mavis Batey. A beautifully illustrated book which will tell you more about the Picturesque and Repton's improvements.